Linda Par

Muffin Cookbook

33 Delicious and Easy Muffin Recipes

Table of Contents

Introduction 6

Double Chocolate Flax Seed Muffins 8

Chocolate Chip Pumpkin Muffins 10

Carrot Cake Muffin Recipe 12

Chocolate Almond Muffins 14

Banana Nut Muffins 16

Carrot-Raisin Muffins 18

Blueberry Muffins 20

Apple Sauce Muffins 22

Whole Wheat Muffins 23

Squash Muffins 25

Peanut Butter Muffins 27

Bacon & Cheese Muffins 29

Blueberry Zucchini Muffins 31

Spiced Apple Muffins 33

Morning Glory Muffins 35

Healthy Cheddar Broccoli Muffins 37

Rhubarb Muffins 39

Spice Muffins 41

Oatmeal Muffins 43

Cheddar Bran Muffins 45

Glazed Doughnut Muffins 47

Ginger Cheese Muffins 50

Banana Muffins 52

Whole Wheat Muffins 54

Honey Muffins 56

Sour Cream Muffins 58

Hawaiian Muffins 60

Scotch Oatmeal Muffins 62

Honey Corn Muffins 64

Maple Corn Muffins 66

Applesauce Oatmeal Muffins 68

Wheat Germ Muffins 70

Date Nut Muffins 72

Conclusion 74

Introduction

All of us are in a rush in the morning. We have to reach the place of work quickly. It's easy to skip the breakfast or stop over for a quick bite at a fast-food joint. Neither of them are good options. The breakfast sets you up for the day. You shouldn't ever skip it. And starting the day with fast-food – that should be the last thing you must do.

And honestly, why settle for any of these two options, when you can grab a home-made muffin? It's healthy, yummy, and can be prepared easily. There are muffins for everybody. And the best part is that you can prepare one easily at home. Minimal baking skills required.

For fruit lovers, there are muffins with bananas and apples. Then there are those made with cheese and butter – wow, they are so yummy. You have to also try the classic blueberry muffins. I can assure you they are irresistible. Take a few for your friends and family. They are going to beg you for more! Then there are some amazing muffins for all chocolate lovers. They are a rage. And don't overlook the cinnamon muffins too. Everyone loves them. Your house is going to smell awesome for hours.

Turn your house into a bakery. Get my awesome muffin recipes, they are all easy to prepare even for the very beginners. I have provided a step-by-step guide on how to prepare each muffin and mentioned what you need for each muffin recipe.

I am sure you will love these incredible muffin recipes. Happy baking!

Double Chocolate Flax Seed Muffins

Get This:

- Whole wheat flour – 1 cup.
- Ground flax seed - ¾ cup.
- Quick-cooking oats - ½ cup.
- Baking soda – 1 teaspoon.
- Baking powder – 1 and ½ teaspoons.
- Cocoa powder - ½ cup.
- Ground cinnamon – 1 tablespoon.
- Chocolate chips - ½ cup.
- Buttermilk or milk – 1 cup.
- Applesauce or pumpkin puree - ¾ cup.
- Brown sugar – 1 cup.
- Egg – 1.
- Vanilla extract – 1 teaspoon.

Do This:

- Preheat the oven to 200 degrees C or 400 degrees F.

- Line with paper muffin liners or grease 12 muffin cups.

- Combine flax seed, flour, baking soda, oats, cocoa powder, baking powder, chocolate chips and cinnamon in a bowl. Beat the pumpkin/applesauce, milk, egg, brown sugar and vanilla in another bowl till it has become smooth. Stir the wet ingredients gently till it has mixed well.

- Now spoon the same amount of batter into the muffin cups.

- Bake till the time you can insert a toothpick in the middle of the muffin and it comes out clean. It should take you between 20 and 30 minutes.

Chocolate Chip Pumpkin Muffins

Get This:

- Wheat flour – 3 cups.
- Sugar - 2 and ½ cups.
- Cinnamon – 1 teaspoon.
- Baking powder – 2 teaspoons.
- Pumpkin – 2 cups.
- Eggs – 4.
- Chocolate chips – 12 oz.
- Oil – 1 cup.
- Water - ½ cup.
- Salt - ½ teaspoon.

Do This:

- Pour all the ingredients into a jar one by one.

- You should pour the water and oil at the last.

- Now mix them carefully till you have a smooth batter.

- Spoon this into your papered or greased muffin cups.

- Bake the cups for 25 minutes. You should bake at 350 degrees.

Carrot Cake Muffin Recipe

Get This:

- Brown sugar - 1 and ½ cups.
- Vegetable oil - ¼ cup.
- Apple sauce - ½ cup.
- Eggs – 3.
- Vanilla extract – 1 teaspoon.
- Buttermilk - ¾ cup.
- Grated carrots - 2 and ½ cups.
- AP flour – 1 cup.
- Whole wheat flour - 1 and ½ cup.
- Oatmeal - ½ cup.
- Flax seed - ¼ cup.
- Baking soda – 2 teaspoons.
-

- Ground cinnamon – 2 teaspoons.
- Salt - 1 and ½ teaspoons.

Do This:

- Pour sugar and the wet ingredients into a large bowl and mix well.
- Add the carrot.
- Now mix the dry ingredients separately.
- Add them to the carrot mixture.
- Pour this to the muffin cups.
- Bake between 20 and 25 minutes.

Chocolate Almond Muffins

Get This:

- Coconut oil - ¼ cup.
- Milk - ¾ cup.
- Vanilla extract – ½ teaspoon.
- Brown sugar – 2/3 cup.
- Almond extract – ½ teaspoon (optional).
- Whole wheat flour - ¾ cup.
- Almond flour - ¼ cup.
- Unsweetened cocoa powder - ¼ cup.
- Salt – ¼ teaspoon.
- Baking powder – 1 teaspoon.

Do This:

- Preheat your oven to 350 degrees F.

- Grease the muffin tin with coconut oil.

- Whisk together the oil, milk, sugar and extracts in a mixing bowl. You will find it difficult to mix the coconut oil. Just use a fork to break up the pieces. You don't have to worry about mixing completely at this stage.

- Stir or whisk the cocoa powder, flours, salt and baking powder in a mixing bowl of medium size.

- Now pour your wet ingredients into the dry content without mixing.

- Pour batter into your muffin tin. Fill a little more than half. The batter needs to be thin. However it shouldn't be completely liquid.

- Bake between 18 and 20 minutes till the time you can insert a toothpick to the center of the muffin and it comes out clean.

- Transfer your muffin to a cooling rack. Let it stay for 20 minutes.

- If you want, you can spread a chocolate icing over the muffin or garnish with almond.

Banana Nut Muffins

Get This:

- Egg – 1.
- Ripe bananas (mashed) – 2.
- Melted butter – 1/3 cup.
- Vanilla – 1 and ½ teaspoons.
- Plain Greek Yogurt – 2 teaspoons.
- Whole wheat flour – 1 and ½ cups.
- Ground flax seed - ¼ cup.
- Brown sugar - ¾ cup.
- Salt – 1 teaspoon.
- Oats - 1/3 cup.
- Baking powder - ½ teaspoon.
- Baking soda - ½ teaspoon.

- Ground cinnamon - ½ teaspoon.
- Chopped pecans - ½ cup.

Do This:

- Line your muffin tin with paper liners.
- Preheat the oven to 350 degrees F.
- Use a fork to mash the bananas. Keep them in a measuring bowl.
- Add the vanilla, egg, yogurt, and melted butter.
- Combine sugar, flour, baking powder, baking soda, salt, nuts and cinnamon in a big bowl.
- Put the wet ingredients into the dry ingredients.
- Lightly spoon out the butter into your muffin pan.
- Keep into the preheated oven and bake for 20 to 25 minutes.

Carrot-Raisin Muffins

Get This:

- Brown sugar – ½ cup.
- Soft butter – ¼ cup.
- Eggs – 2.
- Raisins – ½ cup.
- Flour – 1 and ½ cups.
- Sour cream – 1 cup.
- Shredded carrot – 1 cup.
- Baking soda – 1 teaspoon.
- Flakes and unsweetened coconut – ½ cup.
- Cinnamon – 1 teaspoon.

Do This:

- Preheat the oven to 350 degrees F.

- Beat the butter and sugar together in a big bowl till the time they have mixed well. Beat for 2 minutes.

- Add eggs and sour cream.

- Beat the egg mixture till you have this well mixed.

- Stir in coconut, raisins and carrots.

- Take another medium-sized bowl, and stir together baking soda, cinnamon and flour.

- Now add this second mixture to the sour cream mixture. Stir this to make sure that it blends properly.

- Spoon the mixture to your muffin tins.

- Bake till you have it slightly brown. It should take about 30 minutes.

Blueberry Muffins

Get This:

- Egg – 1.
- Milk – ½ cup.
- Flour – 1 and ½ cup.
- Vegetable oil - ¼ cup.
- Salt – ½ teaspoon.
- Baking powder – 2 teaspoons.
- Sugar – ½ cup.
- Blueberries – 1 cup.

Do This:

- Preheat your oven to 400 degrees F.
- Put the milk, eggs and oil in a big bowl and beat well.
- Now put flour, sugar, salt and baking powder and stir.

- Include the blueberries.

- Bake the muffin between 20 and 25 minutes.

Apple Sauce Muffins

Get This:

- Flax seed - ¼ cup.
- Coconut oil - ¾ cup.
- Brown sugar - 1 and ½ cup.
- Apple sauce (non-sweetened) – 2 cups.
- Baking soda – 2 teaspoons.
- Whole wheat flour – 3 cups.
- Oats – 1 cup.

Do This:

- Take a large bowl and pour everything into it. Mix well.
- Scoop the paste out and put it into papered muffin cups.
- You need to bake at 350 degrees for 20 to 25 minutes.

Whole Wheat Muffins

Get This:

- Whole wheat flour – 1 cup.
- AP flour – 1 cup.
- Flax seed – ¼ cup.
- Brown sugar - ½ cup.
- Baking powder – 2 teaspoons.
- Baking soda – 1 teaspoon.
- Cinnamon – ½ teaspoon.
- Salt – 1 teaspoon.
- Egg – 1.
- Oil – 1 tablespoon.
- Plain yogurt - ¾ cup.
- Vanilla extract – 1 teaspoon.
- Milk – 1 cup.

Do This:

- Preheat your oven to 190 degrees C or 375 degrees F.

- Grease the muffin tin or you can line with paper liners.

- Put all the ingredients into a big bowl and stir.

- Spoon the batter out and place it inside the muffin cups.

- Now bake for 18-20 minutes in your preheated oven.

- Let it stay for 20 minutes for cooling.

Squash Muffins

Get This:

- Flour – 3 cups.
- Baking powder – 4 teaspoons.
- Cinnamon – 1 teaspoon.
- Salt – 1 teaspoon.
- Sugar – ¾ cup.
- Beaten eggs – 2.
- Nutmeg – 1 teaspoon.
- Milk – 1 cup.
- Cooked winter squash – 1 cup.
- Vegetable oil – ½ cup.
- Raisins – 1 cup.

Do This:

- Sift the baking powder, flour, cinnamon, nutmeg and salt together.

- Put in oil, squash, milk and eggs.

- Add your raisins to the flour mixture.

- Add sugar to the egg mixture.

- Now combine the two mixtures and stir well till they have blended nicely.

- Grease your muffin cups and fill 2/3rd.

- Bake for 15 to 20 minutes at 400 degrees. You should have a golden brown color.

Peanut Butter Muffins

Get This:

- Flour – 2 cups.
- Baking powder – 3 tablespoons.
- Salt – ½ teaspoon.
- Sugar – ½ cup.
- Chunky peanut butter – ½ cup.
- Butter – 2 teaspoons.
- Eggs – 2.
- Milk – 1 cup.
- Ground cinnamon – 2 teaspoons.
- Peanut butter – 1 tablespoon.

Do This:

- Put the sugar, salt, baking powder and flour together and stir.

- Include the butter and peanut butter till the mixture looks like coarse crumbs.

- Now put in the eggs and milk together.

- Stir till the time the paste has moistened.

- Fill your greased muffin pans. Fill up $2/3^{rd}$.

- Bake for 15 to 20 minutes at 400 degrees.

- Brush the top of your muffins with 2 tablespoons of melted butter.

- Sprinkle cinnamon and sugar on top.

Bacon & Cheese Muffins

Get This:

- Baking powder – 2 teaspoons.
- Flour – 2 cups.
- Black pepper – ¼ teaspoon.
- Salt – ¼ teaspoon.
- Cooled and melted margarine or butter – ¼ cup.
- Milk – 1 and ¼ cup.
- Egg – 1.
- Degreased, cooked and diced bacon – ½ lb.
- Shredded cheddar cheese – ¾ cup.

Do This:

- Stir together the baking powder, flour, pepper and salt in a big mixing bowl.

- Take a small bowl and mix the melted butter, eggs, margarine and milk.

- Combine the dry and wet ingredients and stir. It should be moistened.

- Fold in the cheese and bacon till it is combined.

- Scoop inside lined or greased muffin tins.

- Now bake this for 20 to 25 minutes at 400 degrees. Bake till you get the golden brown color.

Blueberry Zucchini Muffins

Get This:

- Honey – ¼ cup.
- White wheat flour – 1 and ½ cup.
- Salt – ½ teaspoon.
- Olive oil – 1/3 cup.
- Baking powder – 2 tablespoons.
- Egg – 1.
- Milk – ½ cup.
- Blueberries – 1 cup.
- Vanilla – 1 tablespoon.
- Drained and shredded zucchini – 1 cup.

Do This:

- Shred the zucchini.

- Squeeze the shreds in paper towels or cheesecloth for draining out the excess liquid.

- Put all the dry ingredients into a bowl and mix together.

- Now combine your wet and dry ingredients.

- Keep stirring till your paste is moist.

- Add your zucchini.

- Fold in the blueberries carefully.

- Scoop this into the muffin tins. Fill up 3/4th. You will get 8 muffins.

- Bake for 15 to 20 minutes at 375 degrees. If your muffin tins are larger in size, then bake for 5 more minutes.

Spiced Apple Muffins

Get This:

- Well beaten eggs – 2.
- Flour – 3 cups.
- Milk – 1 and ¼ cups.
- Baking powder – 4 teaspoons.
- Salt – 2 teaspoons.
- Sugar – 3 tablespoons.
- Chopped apples – 1 cup.
- Cinnamon – ¼ teaspoon.

Do This:

- Preheat your oven to 420 degrees.
- Mix the baking powder, flour, salt and sugar.
- Stir in milk and eggs.

- Now add the apples.

- Spoon out the mixture and put into the muffin tins.

- Mix together the cinnamon and 2 tablespoons of sugar.

- Sprinkle this mixture on top of your muffins.

- Bake them for 25 minutes.

Morning Glory Muffins

Get This:

- Flour – 2 cups.
- Raisins – ½ cup.
- Baking soda – 2 teaspoons.
- Sugar – 1 cup.
- Salt – ½ teaspoon.
- Eggs – 3.
- Cinnamon – 2 teaspoons.
- Vegetable oil – 1/3 cup.
- Vanilla – 2 teaspoons.
- Grated carrots – 2 cups.
- Applesauce – 1/3 cup.
- Sliced almonds – ½ cup.

- Shredded coconut - ½ cup.

- Grated green apple – 1 large.

Do This:

- Preheat your oven to 350 degrees.

- Soak the raisins in hot water for half an hour. Drain the water out.

- Mix sugar, flour, cinnamon, salt and baking soda.

- Now stir in the coconut, almonds, apple, carrots, and raisins.

- Beat the applesauce, vanilla, eggs and oil together.

- Stir this into the first mixture. You need everything combined well.

- Bake your muffin for 20 to 25 minutes.

- Let it stay for some time for cooling.

Healthy Cheddar Broccoli Muffins

Get This:

- Egg whites – 4.
- Skim milk – 2/3 cup.
- Oil – ¼ cup.
- Chopped scallion – ¼ cup.
- Chopped frozen broccoli – 1 and ½ cup.
- Shredded cheddar cheese – 1 cup.
- Toasted pine nuts – ¼ cup.
- Flour – 1 and ¼ cup.
- Sugar – 2 tablespoon.
- Baking powder – 2 and ½ tablespoon.
- Pepper – ½ tablespoon.
- Kosher salt – 1 pinch.
- Shredded Parmesan cheese - ½ cup.

Do This:

- Heat your oven to 400 degrees.

- Grease the muffin tin with some nonstick cooking spray.

- Now combine the oil, eggs and milk.

- Add the pine nuts, scallion and broccoli.

- Stir the cheese. Leave a little bit of cheese for the topping.

- Add the baking powder, flour, pepper, salt and sugar.

- Fill your muffin tins equally.

- Now sprinkle the remaining portion of cheese on your muffin.

- Bake between 30 and 35 minutes. The top will have distinct brown color.

Rhubarb Muffins

Get This:

- Vegetable oil – ½ cup.
- Brown sugar – 1 and ¼ cup.
- Vanilla – 2 teaspoons.
- Egg – 1.
- Chopped nuts – ½ cup.
- Diced rhubarb – 1 and ½ cup.
- Buttermilk – 1 cup.
- Flour – 2 and ½ cup.
- Baking soda – 1 teaspoon.
- Baking powder – 1 teaspoon.
- Melted butter – 1 tablespoon.
- Cinnamon – 1 teaspoon.
- Salt – ½ teaspoon.

Do This:

- Preheat your oven to 400 degrees.

- Bring together the egg, oil, sugar, buttermilk and vanilla in a big bowl. Beat this well.

- Stir in the nuts and rhubarb.

- Take another bowl and stir together baking powder, baking soda, flour, and salt.

- Stir into the rhubarb mixture.

- Now fill your muffin pans $2/3^{rd}$.

- Sprinkle the toppings.

- Bake between 20 and 25 minutes.

Spice Muffins

Get This:

- Well beaten eggs – 1.
- Flour – 2 cups.
- Milk – 1 cup.
- Sugar – ½ cup.
- Melted butter – ¼ cup.
- Cinnamon, nutmeg, and ginger – 1 teaspoon each.
- Baking powder – 3 teaspoons.
- Salt – 1 teaspoon.

Do This:

- Preheat your oven to 425 degrees.
- Include the shortening, milk, sugar and egg.
- Add the dry ingredients.

- Beat this till you have a smooth paste.

- Fill the muffin tins 2/3rd.

- Now bake between 15 and 20 minutes.

Oatmeal Muffins

Get This:

- Sugar – ¼ cup.
- Flour – 1 cup.
- Uncooked oats – 1 cup.
- Baking powder – 1 tablespoon.
- Vegetable oil – 3 tablespoons.
- Beaten egg – 1.
- Salt – ½ tablespoon.
- Nonfat milk – 1 cup.

Do This:

- Pour the baking powder, flour, sugar and salt into a bowl.
- Include the oats and stir.

- Add the egg, nonfat milk and vegetable oil.

- Keep stirring till all the dry ingredients are moistened.

- Fill your muffin cups 2/3rd.

- Bake for 15 minutes and 425 degrees.

Cheddar Bran Muffins

Get This:

- Whole bran – 1 cup.
- Buttermilk – 1 and ¼ cup.
- Sugar – 1/3 cup.
- Shortening – ¼ cup.
- Egg – 1.
- Flour – 1 and ½ cup.
- Salt – ½ teaspoon.
- Baking powder – 1 and ½ cup.
- Grated cheddar cheese – 1 cup.
- Baking soda – ¼ teaspoon.

Do This:

- Preheat the oven to 400 degrees.

- Now take a small bowl and pour the buttermilk over bran. Let it sit so that the bran can soften.

- Sugar and cream shortening till it gets fluffy and light.

- Beat in the egg.

- Sift together baking powder, baking soda, flour and salt.

- Alternatively add the bran mixture and milk to the creamed mixture.

- Stir in the cheese.

- Fill up the greased muffin pans 2/3rd.

- Bake for 30 minutes.

Glazed Doughnut Muffins

Get This:

- Butter – ¼ cup.
- Granulated sugar – ½ cup.
- Vegetable oil – ¼ cup.
- Brown sugar – 1/3 cup.
- Baking powder – 1 and ½ teaspoon.
- Baking soda – ¼ teaspoon.
- Eggs – 2.
- Cinnamon – 1 teaspoon.
- Ground nutmeg – 1 teaspoon.
- Vanilla extract – 1 teaspoon.
- Flour – 2 and 2/3 cups.
- Salt – ¾ teaspoon.
- Milk – 1 cup.

Do This:

- Preheat your oven to 425 degrees F.

- Line the muffin cups or grease the tins.

- Take a medium sized mixing bowl and bring together the vegetable oil, sugars, and butter.

- Beat the eggs as you include them.

- Stir in baking soda, baking powder, cinnamon, nutmeg, vanilla and salt.

- Stir the flour to your butter mixture alternatively with milk. Start and end with flour. Everything needs to combine thoroughly.

- Spoon out the batter into the pan. Fill the cups almost completely.

- Now bake your muffins for 15 to 20 minutes. The color should turn golden brown. Insert a cake tester to check. It should come out clean.

- Now take a medium bowl and mix together the vanilla, confectioners' sugar, melted butter, and some water. Keep whisking till it is smooth.

- Dip the muffin crown into the glaze when your muffins are somewhat cool. Let the glaze harden.

Ginger Cheese Muffins

Get This:

- Baking soda – ¼ teaspoon.
- Baking powder – 3 teaspoons.
- Flour – 2 cups.
- Salt – ½ teaspoon.
- Ginger – ½ teaspoon.
- Milk – ½ cup.
- Well beaten egg – 1.
- Melted butter – 4 tablespoons.
- Molasses – ½ cup.
- Grated cheddar cheese – ¾ cup.

Do This:

- Preheat your oven to 425 degrees.

- Sift together all the dry ingredients.

- Include the molasses, milk and egg.

- Now add this to the dry ingredients as you stir persistently.

- Beat till it is smooth.

- Stir in the cheese and add butter.

- Fill the muffin pans. They should be 2/3rd full.

- Bake between 10 and 15 minutes.

Banana Muffins

Get This:

- Baking powder – 2 and ½ teaspoons.
- Flour – 2 cups.
- Butter – ½ cup.
- Salt – ½ teaspoon.
- Eggs – 2.
- Sugar – 1 cup.
- Vanilla – 1 teaspoon.
- Ripe and mashed banana – 1 and ½ cups.
- Sugar – 1 tablespoon.
- Milk – ¼ cup.
- Cinnamon – ½ teaspoon.

Do This:

- Preheat your oven to 375 degrees.

- Include salt, baking powder and flour and combine well.

- Take another bowl. Include the sugar and butter till it is fluffy and light.

- Add the 2 eggs one at a time. Beat them in vanilla.

- Include milk and bananas.

- Stir flour into the egg mixture with the bananas in low speed. Keep stirring till they are combined well.

- Now fill the muffin pans – they should be $2/3^{rd}$ full.

- Sprinkle cinnamon and sugar over the muffins.

- Bake between 20 and 25 minutes.

- Let it stay for 10 minutes for cooling.

Whole Wheat Muffins

Get This:

- Milk – 1 cup.
- Flour – 1 cup.
- Sugar – 2 tablespoons.
- Whole wheat flour – 1 cup.
- Beaten egg – 1.
- Melted shortening – 3 tablespoons.
- Salt – 1 teaspoon.
- Baking powder – 4 tablespoons.

Do This:

- Sift the flour.
- Add sugar, salt, wheat flour and baking powder.
- Combine milk, shortening and egg.

- Pour this into the flour. Keep stirring till it has moistened. Don't beat.

- Grease the muffin tins and fill 2/3rd.

- Bake between 20 and 25 minutes at 400 degrees.

Honey Muffins

Get This:

- Salt – 1 teaspoon.
- Flour – 2 cups.
- Milk – 1 cup
- Baking powder – 3 teaspoons.
- Beaten egg – 1.
- Honey – 4 tablespoons.
- Melted butter – ¼ cup.

Do This:

- Preheat your oven to 400 degrees.
- Sift all the dry ingredients.
- Combine the butter, egg, honey and milk.
- Add them to the flour mixture.

- Stir to moisten the ingredients.

- Fill up your muffin pans ½.

- Bake between 25 and 30 minutes.

Sour Cream Muffins

Get This:

- Baking powder – 1 teaspoon.
- Flour – 1 and 1/3 cup.
- Baking soda – ½ teaspoon.
- Salt – ½ teaspoon.
- Well beaten egg – 1.
- Sugar – 2 tablespoons.
- Sour cream – 1 cup.
- Softened butter – 1 tablespoon.

Do This:

- Sift all the dry ingredients.
- Stir together the sour cream, butter and egg. You have to blend them well.

- Now add the dry ingredients. Stir till it becomes moistened.

- Fill the greased muffin pans ½.

- Bake for 20 to 25 minutes and 400 degrees.

Hawaiian Muffins

Get This:

- Baking powder – 2 tablespoons.
- Flour – 4 cups.
- Salt – 1 tablespoon.
- Sugar – ½ cup.
- Milk – 1 and ½ cup.
- Beaten egg – 4.
- Drained and crushed pineapple – 1 and ½ cup.
- Melted butter – ½ cup.

Do This:

- Sift all the dry ingredients.
- Include the butter, milk and eggs.
- Stir till this becomes smooth.

- Now add the pineapple. Mix this well.

- Grease your muffin pans and scoop out. Fill 3/4th.

- Bake for 20 to 25 minutes and 425 degrees.

Scotch Oatmeal Muffins

Get This:

- Buttermilk – 1 cup.

- Oats – 1 cup.

- Baking powder – 1 tablespoon

- Flour – 1 cup.

- Salt – ½ tablespoon.

- Beaten egg – 1.

- Baking soda – ½ tablespoon.

- Vegetable oil – 1/3 cup.

- Brown sugar - 1/3 cup.

- Chopped raisins, nuts or dates – ¾ cup.

Do This:

- Preheat your oven to 400 degrees.

- Stir the buttermilk, oats, salt, baking soda and baking powder. You need to blend everything well.

- Add the sugar.

- Stir in oil and brown sugar.

- Include the raisins, nuts or dates.

- Stir till everything blends nicely.

- Fill the greased muffin pans 2/3rd.

- Bake for 20 minutes.

Honey Corn Muffins

Get This:

- Flour – ½ cup.
- Yellow cornmeal – ½ cup.
- Baking powder – 2 tablespoon.
- Molasses or honey – 2 tablespoon.
- Salt – ½ tablespoon.
- Egg – 1.
- Milk – ½ cup.
- Vegetable oil – 2 tablespoon.

Do This:

- Sift and mix all the dry ingredients.
- Include the milk and egg.
- Now stir this in oil.

- Scoop this into your greased muffin tins.

- Bake for 17 to 20 minutes at 425 degrees.

Maple Corn Muffins

Get This:

- Cornmeal – 2/3 cup.
- Flour – 1 and 1/3 cup.
- Baking powder – 3 tablespoon.
- Salt – ½ tablespoon.
- Milk – 2/3 cup.
- Eggs – 2.
- Oil or melted shortening – ½ cup.
- Maple syrup – 1/3 cup.

Do This:

- Mix all your dry ingredients and keep this aside.
- Beat the eggs.

- Include the shortening, syrup and milk. Blend everything well.

- Now include the dry ingredients and mix to moisten.

- Spoon this to your greased muffin tins.

- Bake for 25 minutes at 425 degrees.

Applesauce Oatmeal Muffins

Get This:

- Cinnamon – ¾ teaspoon.
- Oats – 1 and ½ cup.
- Vegetable oil – 3 tablespoon.
- Baking soda – ¾ tablespoon.
- Baking powder – 1 tablespoon.
- Flour – 1 and ¼ cup.
- Milk – ½ cup.
- Brown sugar – ½ cup.
- Applesauce – 1 cup.
- Egg white – 1.

Do This:

- Preheat your oven to 400 degrees.

- Mix the cinnamon, flour, oats, baking soda, and baking powder.

- Add egg white, applesauce, milk, oil and brown sugar.

- Blend everything well and scoop to your muffin tins.

- Bake for 20 minutes.

Wheat Germ Muffins

Get This:

- Baking powder – 1 tablespoon.
- Sifted flour – 1 cup.
- Salt – 1 and ½ tablespoon.
- Wheat germ – ½ cup.
- Honey – ¼ cup.
- Beaten egg – 1.
- Oats – ½ cup.
- Oil – ¼ cup.
- Dates – 1 cup.
- Milk – ¾ cup.

Do This:

- Sift together the baking powder, salt and flour.

- Include the other ingredients and stir well until everything is moistened.

- Now spoon to your greased muffin tins.

- Bake for 20 minutes at 400 degrees.

Date Nut Muffins

Get This:

- All Bran cereal – 1 and ½ cup.
- Flour – 1 and ¼ cup.
- Baking powder – 3 tablespoon.
- Milk – 1 cup.
- Egg – 1.
- Sugar – 1/3 cup.
- Salt – 1 tablespoon.
- Finely chopped dates – ½ cup.
- Vegetable oil or melted shortening – ¼ cup.
- Chopped nuts – 1/3 cup.

Do This:

- Add All Bran and milk and let it stay for 5 minutes.
- Include sugar, oil and beaten egg.
- Sift the baking powder, salt and flour.
- Add this to the first mixture.
- Fold in the nuts and dates.
- Scoop to your greased muffin tins.
- Bake for 20 minutes at 400 degrees.

Conclusion

Thank you again for buying this book!

I hope you were able to get some awesome muffin recipes in this book. Hopefully, I was able to show you how you can easily prepare these muffins at home, all by yourself. I have tried to keep it simple by providing step-by-step guidance, and by clearly mentioning the ingredients you need for each muffin recipe.

Muffins can be healthy, yummy, and easy to prepare food. And there's a huge variety you can choose from as well so you could easily prepare all types of muffins at home. You can never get tired of them. Have a muffin for your breakfast or as a snack between meals. Prepare a box of muffins and gift it to your friends and family. They are going to ask for more – you can be sure of that.

Good luck!

Linda Parker

Printed in Great Britain
by Amazon